Telling Time
Math Workbook

Grade 1
For ages 6-7

This book belongs to

_____

Includes:
To the Hour
Half Hour
Quarter Hour
Five Minute Intervals
Word Problems
Practice Sheets

JAYCLAD PUBLISHING

Printed in the United States of America

First Printing, 2017

ISBN 978-1-947343-00-9

Jayclad Publishing
P O Box No: 5279
Kendall Park NJ 08824

www.Jaycladpublishing.com

Fun Facts
Inventor Galileo made a life-changing observation as he attended a church service and noticed a swinging lantern. The lantern gave him the idea that a pendulum could be used to accurately measure time, increasing the future of timekeeping immensely.

The Basics of Telling Time

➲There are 60 seconds in one minute.

➲There are 60 minutes in one hour.

➲There are 24 hours in one day.

➲There are two main hands on a clock, the hour hand and the minute hand.

➲The minute hand is longer than the hour hand.

➲The hour hand makes 2 rotations in 1 day (24 hours).

➲The minute hand makes 24 rotations in 1 day (24 hours).

➲The hour hand and the minute hand rotate clockwise.

The hands of a clock always rotate in the <u>clockwise direction.</u>

60 Seconds = 1 Minute
60 Minutes = 1 Hour
24 Hours = 1 Day

1. There are _____ seconds in one minute.

2. There are _____ minutes in one hour.

3. There are _____ hours in one Day.

4. There are two main hands in a clock, the _____ hand and the _____ hand.

5. The minute hand is _____ than the hour hand.

6. The hour hand makes _____ rotations in 1 day (24 hours).

7. The minute hand makes _____ rotations in 1 day (24 hours).

8. The hour hand and the minute hand rotate in the _____ direction.

Which direction does the hands of a clock rotate? Check the box.

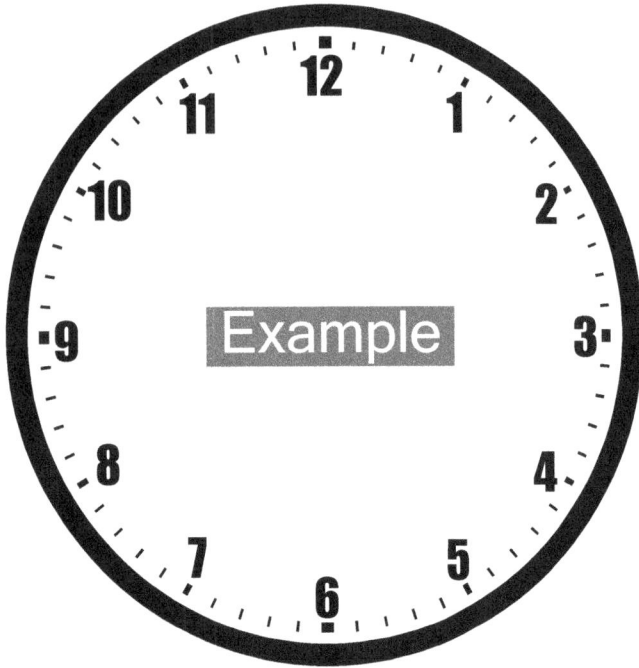

Example

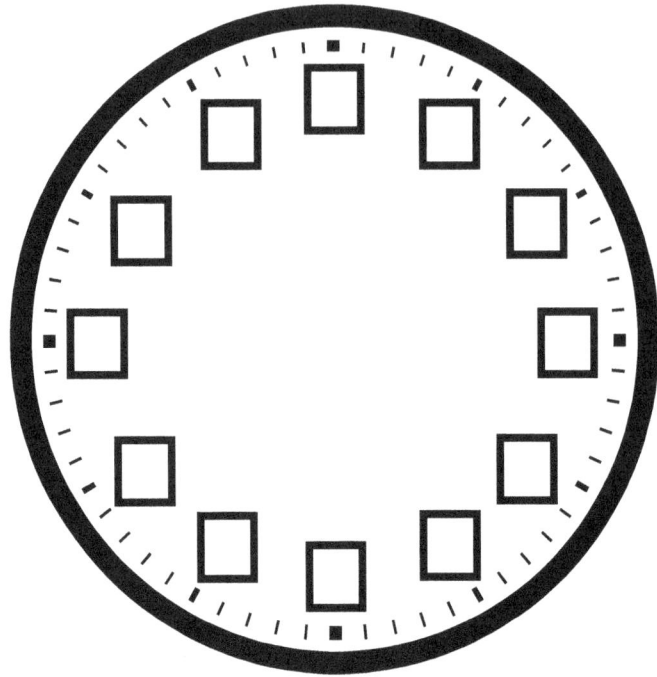

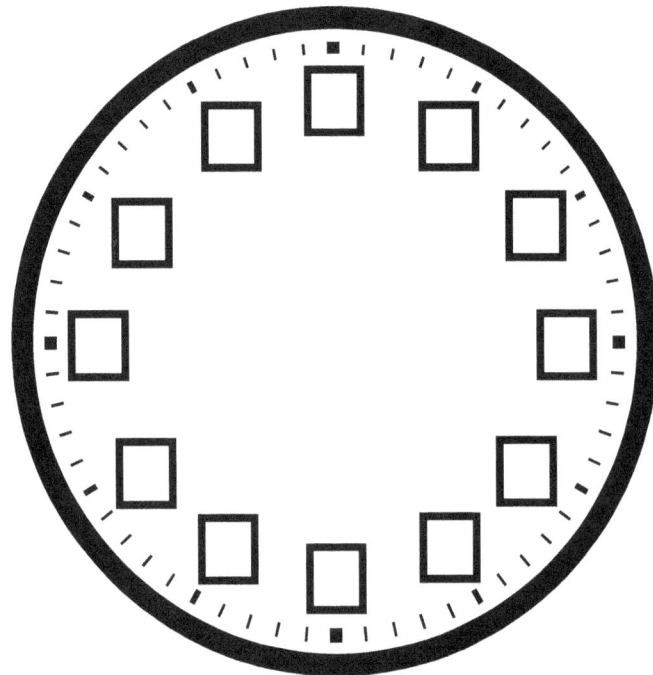

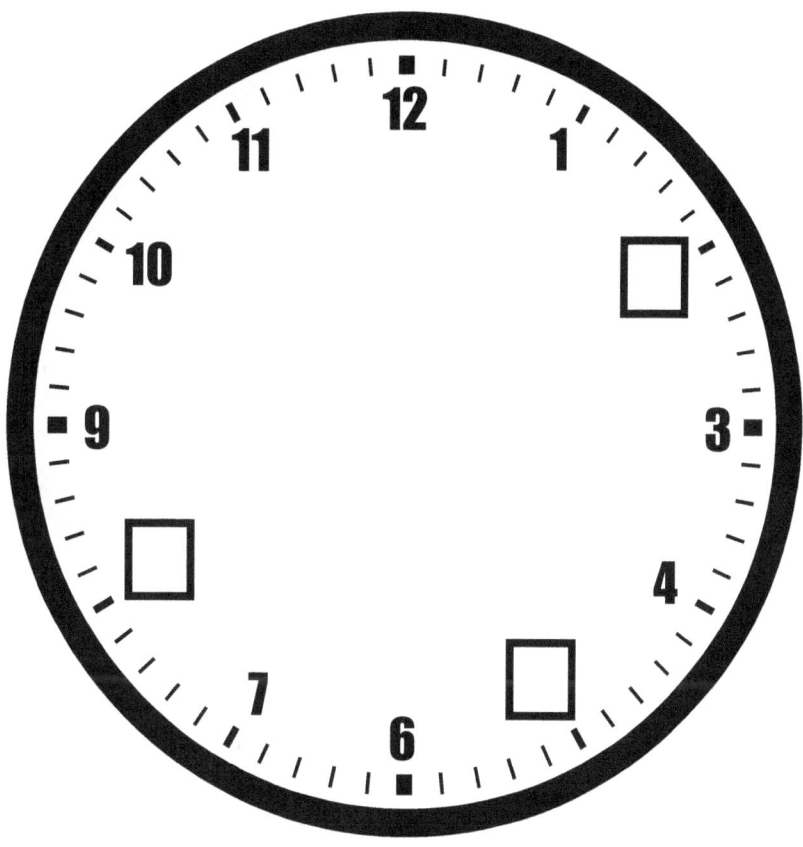

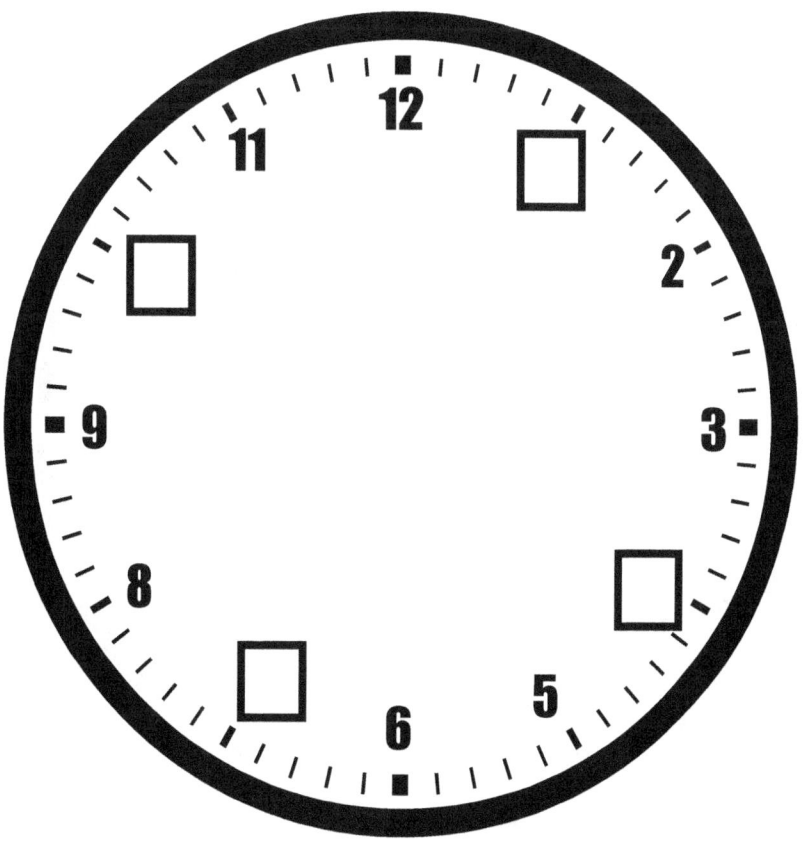

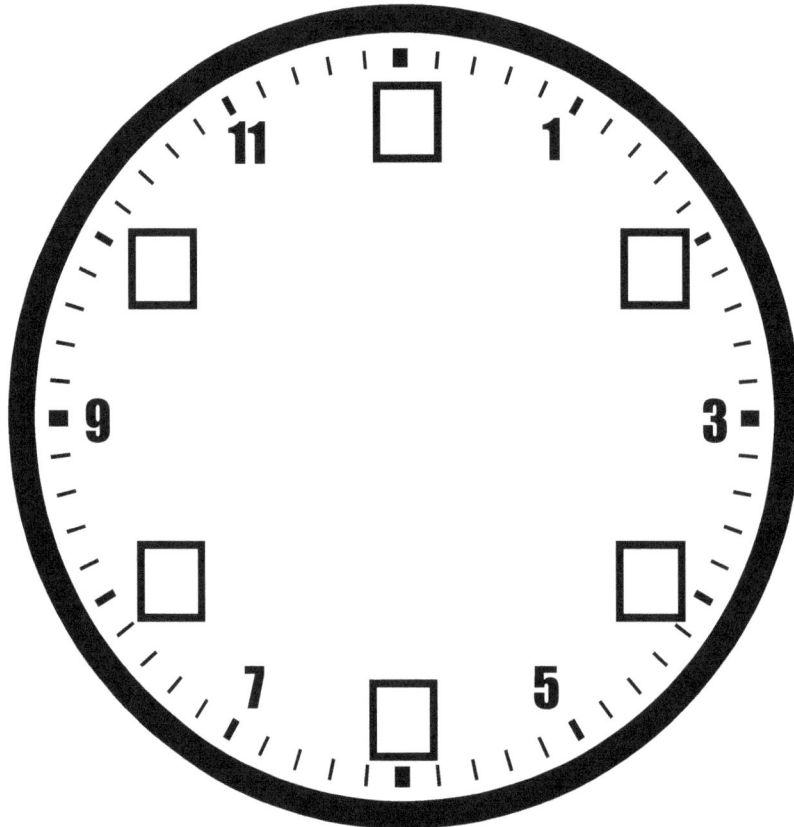

The shorter hand is the hour hand.

The longer hand is the minute hand.

The hour hand is at 1.

The minute hand is at 12.

The time is 1 o'clock

The hour hand is at 5.

The minute hand is at 12.

The time is 5 o'clock

The hour hand is at 9.

The minute hand is at 12.

The time is 9 o'clock

The shorter hand is the hour hand

The longer hand is the minute hand

The hour hand is at ☐

The minute mand is at 12

The time is ☐ o'clock

The hour hand is at ☐

The minute hand is at 12

The time is ☐ o'clock

The hour hand is at ☐

The minute hand is at 12

The time is ☐ o'clock

Choose the Correct Time

Example

☐ 3:00
☑ 10:00
☐ 12:00
☐ 4:00

☐ 8:00
☐ 9:00
☐ 6:00
☐ 4:00

☐ 5:00
☐ 7:00
☐ 12:00
☐ 9:00

☐ 3:00
☐ 7:00
☐ 12:00
☐ 4:00

☐ 4:00
☐ 7:00
☐ 9:00
☐ 1:00

☐ 9:00
☐ 8:00
☐ 5:00
☐ 4:00

☐ 3:00
☐ 7:00
☐ 12:00
☐ 4:00

Choose the Correct Time

GIFTED

1.
- ☐ 2:00
- ☐ 10:00
- ☐ 8:00
- ☐ 11:00

2.
- ☐ 8:00
- ☐ 7:00
- ☐ 12:00
- ☐ 1:00

3.
- ☐ 2:00
- ☐ 9:00
- ☐ 8:00
- ☐ 4:00

4.
- ☐ 5:00
- ☐ 7:00
- ☐ 12:00
- ☐ 9:00

5.
- ☐ 9:00
- ☐ 8:00
- ☐ 5:00
- ☐ 4:00

6.
- ☐ 8:00
- ☐ 9:00
- ☐ 6:00
- ☐ 4:00

7.
- ☐ 4:00
- ☐ 7:00
- ☐ 9:00
- ☐ 1:00

8.
- ☐ 3:00
- ☐ 7:00
- ☐ 12:00
- ☐ 1:00

Choose the Correct Time

Clock 1
- ☐ 6:00
- ☐ 10:00
- ☐ 9:00
- ☐ 12:00

Clock 2
- ☐ 3:00
- ☐ 7:00
- ☐ 12:00
- ☐ 2:00

Clock 3
- ☐ 8:00
- ☐ 9:00
- ☐ 2:00
- ☐ 4:00

Clock 4
- ☐ 5:00
- ☐ 7:00
- ☐ 12:00
- ☐ 9:00

Clock 5
- ☐ 3:00
- ☐ 7:00
- ☐ 12:00
- ☐ 4:00

Clock 6
- ☐ 3:00
- ☐ 10:00
- ☐ 12:00
- ☐ 4:00

Clock 7
- ☐ 3:00
- ☐ 7:00
- ☐ 12:00
- ☐ 4:00

Clock 8
- ☐ 5:00
- ☐ 7:00
- ☐ 12:00
- ☐ 9:00

Draw the Hour Hand

Example

`9:00`

If the time is 9 o'clock, The hour hand should point to 9.

The hour hand is shorter than the minute hand.

`6:00`

`11:00`

`10:00`

`7:00`

`12:00`

`8:00`

`2:00`

`3:00`

`1:00`

Draw the Hour Hand

`10:00`

`5:00`

`7:00`

`3:00`

`1:00`

`9:00`

`4:00`

`2:00`

`8:00`

`12:00`

`6:00`

`11:00`

4:00

9:00

5:00

1:00

2:00

3:00

10:00

6:00

11:00

8:00

7:00

12:00

4:00 | Example

7:00

11:00

3:00

Circle the Correct Answer

1.00

2.00

9.00

6.00

Circle the Correct Answer

5:00

8:00

10.00

12.00

Seven o'clock

 Draw the Hour and Minute Hand

Example

9:00

Note
The shorter hand is the hour hand.
The longer hand is the minute hand.
The hour hand is at 9.
The minute hand is at 12.

7:00

2:00

5:00

1:00

8:00

6:00

11:00

10:00

3:00

Draw the Hour and Minute Hand

8:00

11:00

3:00

7:00

4:00

9:00

2:00

6:00

5:00

10:00

12:00

1:00

Draw the Hour and Minute Hand

4:00

10:00

6:00

2:00

7:00

5:00

8:00

1:00

3:00

11:00

12:00

Great Job!

Nine o'clock

Seven o'clock

Six o'clock

Eleven o'clock

Four o'clock

Two o'clock

One o'clock

Eight o'clock

Word Problems

? Alisha wakes up everyday at 6 o'clock. Draw the time on the clock when she will wake up.

? Dev leaves for school at 9 o'clock everyday. Which of the clocks shows the time that he should leave for school.

☐　　　　☐　　　　☐

? Lyn goes to bed at 10 o'clock every night. Draw the time on the clock when Lyn will go to bed.

? Mike eats lunch at 12 o'clock and eats his dinner at 6 o'clock. Which of the clocks shows the time when he will eat his dinner.

☐

☐

☐

? Wendy started her homework at 3 o'clock. It took her 2 Hours to finish the homework. What time did she finish her homework. Draw the time on the clock and write the answer.

Answer _____

? Bill wakes up every day at 6 o'clock. Today he was 1 hour late. What time did we wake up?. Draw the time on the clock and write the answer.

Answer _____

Explanation of Half Hour

The shorter hand is the hour hand.

The longer hand is the minute hand.

The hour hand is in the middle of 7 and 8.

The minute hand is at 6.

The time is half past seven.

The hour hand is in the middle of 1 and 2.

The minute hand is at 6.

The time is half past one.

The hour hand is in the middle of 5 and 6.

The minute hand is at 6.

The time is half past five.

The shorter hand is the hour hand.

The longer hand is the minute hand.

The hour hand is in the middle of ☐ and ☐

The minute hand is at 6

The time is half past two.

The hour hand is in the middle of ☐ and ☐

The minute hand is at ☐

The time is half past eleven.

The hour hand is in the middle of ☐ and ☐

The minute hand is at ☐

The time is half past ☐

Clock 1:
- ☐ 3:30
- ☐ 10:30
- ☐ 12:30
- ☐ 4:30

Clock 2:
- ☐ 8:30
- ☐ 7:30
- ☐ 12:30
- ☐ 1:30

Clock 3:
- ☐ 8:30
- ☐ 9:30
- ☐ 6:30
- ☐ 4:30

Clock 4:
- ☐ 5:30
- ☐ 7:30
- ☐ 12:30
- ☐ 9:30

Clock 5:
- ☐ 3:30
- ☐ 2:30
- ☐ 12:30
- ☐ 4:30

Clock 6:
- ☐ 10:30
- ☐ 7:30
- ☐ 9:30
- ☐ 1:30

Clock 7:
- ☐ 9:30
- ☐ 8:30
- ☐ 5:30
- ☐ 11:30

Clock 8:
- ☐ 6:30
- ☐ 1:30
- ☐ 9:30
- ☐ 8:30

Clock 1:
- ☐ 3:30
- ☐ 10:30
- ☐ 9:30
- ☐ 4:30

Clock 2:
- ☐ 1:30
- ☐ 7:30
- ☐ 12:30
- ☐ 5:30

Clock 3:
- ☐ 8:30
- ☐ 9:30
- ☐ 5:30
- ☐ 4:30

Clock 4:
- ☐ 3:30
- ☐ 7:30
- ☐ 12:30
- ☐ 9:30

Clock 5:
- ☐ 3:30
- ☐ 6:30
- ☐ 12:30
- ☐ 4:30

Clock 6:
- ☐ 8:30
- ☐ 7:30
- ☐ 9:30
- ☐ 1:30

Clock 7:
- ☐ 12:30
- ☐ 8:30
- ☐ 5:30
- ☐ 4:30

Clock 8:
- ☐ 3:30
- ☐ 7:30
- ☐ 2:30
- ☐ 9:30

Choose the Correct Time

1.
- ☐ 3:30
- ☐ 10:30
- ☐ 12:30
- ☐ 8:30

2.
- ☐ 3:30
- ☐ 10:30
- ☐ 12:30
- ☐ 1:30

3.
- ☐ 8:30
- ☐ 9:30
- ☐ 6:30
- ☐ 4:30

4.
- ☐ 5:30
- ☐ 12:30
- ☐ 12:30
- ☐ 3:30

5.
- ☐ 3:30
- ☐ 7:30
- ☐ 4:30
- ☐ 6:30

6.
- ☐ 5:30
- ☐ 11:30
- ☐ 9:30
- ☐ 1:30

7.
- ☐ 9:30
- ☐ 11:30
- ☐ 5:30
- ☐ 4:30

8.
- ☐ 3:30
- ☐ 2:30
- ☐ 12:30
- ☐ 7:30

Draw the Hour Hand

Example

9:30

If the time is 9:30, the hour hand should point between 9 and 10.

The hour hand is shorter than the minute hand.

3:30

1:30

7:30

4:30

2:30

8:30

12:30

6:30

11:30

9:30

5:30

4:30

6:30

11:30

10:30

7:30

12:30

8:30

2:30

3:30

1:30

GIFTED

4:30

9:30

5:30

1:30

2:30

3:30

10:30

6:30

11:30

8:30

7:30

12:30

Circle the Correct Answer

4:30 Example

7:30

11:30

3:30

Circle the Correct Answer

1:30

2:30

9:30

6:30

Circle the Correct Answer

5:30

8:30

10:30

12:30

GIFTED

Half past nine

GIFTED

Draw the Hour and Minute Hand

Example

4:30

When the time is 4:30, The hour hand should point between 4 and 5, the minute hand should point to 6.

2:30

7:30

5:30

8:30

1:30

3:30

10:30

12:30

9:30

9:30

12:30

4:30

7:30

2:30

5:30

1:30

8:30

6:30

11:30

10:30

3:30

Draw the Hour and Minute Hand

8:30

11:30

3:30

7:30

4:30

9:30

2:30

6:30

5:30

10:30

12:30

1:30

Match the Correct Answers

Half past four

Half past eight

Half past one

Half past eleven

Half past six

Half past nine

Half past three

Half past twelve

? Derek's bus reaches school at half past nine. Which of the clocks shows the time when Derek will reach school.

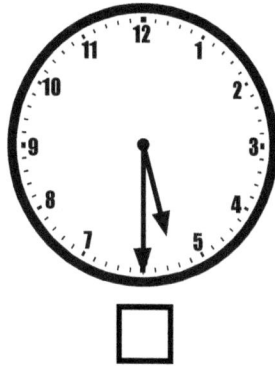

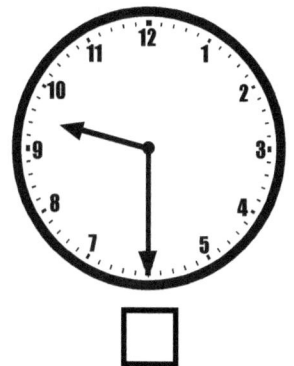

☐   ☐   ☐

? Alisha wakes up at 6 o'clock every day. Today, she is late by 30 minutes. Draw the time on the clock when Alisha woke up today and write the answer.

Answer _____

? Lisa does her homework at half past seven. Which of the clocks shows the time when Lisa will do her homework.

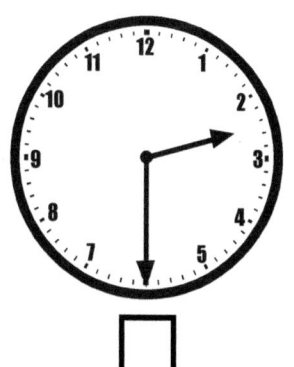

☐   ☐   ☐

Word Problems

? Joe started his lunch at 12 o'clock. It took him 30 minutes to eat his lunch. What time did he finish his lunch. Draw the time on the clock and write the answer.

Answer _____

? Alisha watches TV every day at half past six. Draw the time on the clock when Alisha will watch TV

? The present time is 8 o'clock. What time will it be 30 minutes from now. Draw and write the answer.

Answer _____

Quarter Past and Quarter To

The minute hand is pointing to 3

The hour hand is not pointing to 4, but slightly past 4.

Time is quarter past four
or
4:15

The minute hand is pointing to 9

The hour hand is not pointing to 5, but slightly before 5.

Time is quarter to five
or
4:45

The minute hand is at ☐

The hour hand is slightly after 8

The time is quarter past eight
or
8:15

The minute hand is at ☐

The hour hand is slightly after ☐

The time is quarter past three
or
3:15

The minute hand is at ☐

The hour hand is slightly after ☐

The time is quarter past ☐

or 1: ☐

The minute hand is at ☐

The hour hand is slightly before 8

The time is quarter to eight
or
7:45

The minute hand is at ☐

The hour hand is slightly before ☐

The time is quarter to one
or
12:45

The minute hand is at ☐

The hour hand is slightly before ☐

The time is quarter to ☐

or 2:☐

Choose the Correct Time

Clock 1:
- ☐ 2:15
- ☐ 7:45
- ☐ 8:15
- ☐ 6:15

Clock 2:
- ☐ 4:15
- ☐ 3:45
- ☐ 2:15
- ☐ 4:15

Clock 3:
- ☐ 11:15
- ☐ 5:45
- ☐ 9:15
- ☐ 11:45

Clock 4:
- ☐ 1:15
- ☐ 2:30
- ☐ 4:45
- ☐ 6:30

Clock 5:
- ☐ 7:45
- ☐ 10:30
- ☐ 4:45
- ☐ 9:45

Clock 6:
- ☐ 4:45
- ☐ 7:45
- ☐ 9:45
- ☐ 1:45

Clock 7:
- ☐ 2:30
- ☐ 8:15
- ☐ 6:45
- ☐ 4:15

Clock 8:
- ☐ 3:45
- ☐ 7:15
- ☐ 12:45
- ☐ 4:45

1.
- ☐ 1:15
- ☐ 7:45
- ☐ 8:45
- ☐ 12:45

2.
- ☐ 3:45
- ☐ 7:15
- ☐ 12:25
- ☐ 11:15

3.
- ☐ 8:20
- ☐ 9:15
- ☐ 6:15
- ☐ 4:15

4.
- ☐ 5:25
- ☐ 7:45
- ☐ 7:15
- ☐ 9:10

5.
- ☐ 5:45
- ☐ 2:45
- ☐ 11:15
- ☐ 2:20

6.
- ☐ 8:35
- ☐ 7:15
- ☐ 5:15
- ☐ 2:20

7.
- ☐ 3:05
- ☐ 1:45
- ☐ 9:15
- ☐ 10:45

8.
- ☐ 4:15
- ☐ 2:55
- ☐ 9:25
- ☐ 3:45

Write the Time in Words

Quarter past one

Quarter to two

Write the Time in Words

Example

Quarter to Twelve

The minute hand points to 9 and the hour hand is close to 12.

Quarter past ten

Quarter to two

Quarter to eleven

Quarter past one

Quarter past eleven

Quarter to six

Draw the Minute Hand

GIFTED

Quarter to five

Quarter to ten

Quarter past four

Quarter past nine

Quarter past two

Quarter past eight

Quarter to nine

Quarter to eight

Quarter to three

Quarter to seven

Quarter past three

Quarter past twelve

Quarter to one

Quarter past seven

Quarter past five

Quarter past six

Quarter past four   3:15

Quarter to seven   11:45

Quarter past six   2:15

Quarter to twelve   1:45

Quarter past nine   4:15

Quarter to two   3:45

Quarter past three   10:45

Quarter to four   6:45

Quarter past two   6:15

Quarter to eleven   9:15

5:45 | **Example**

5:15

10:15

12:45

Circle the Correct Answer

12:15

2:45

3:15

9:45

GIFTED

P

Example

Quarter to three

Pay close attention to the hour and minute hand. Note that the hour hand is not at 3 when the time is quarter to three, but close to 3

Quarter to one

Quarter to five

Quarter past one

Quarter past eleven

Quarter to four

Quarter to nine

Quarter past nine

Quarter to eight

Quarter past eight

Quarter to four

Quarter past seven

Quarter to ten

Quarter to eleven

Quarter past three

Quarter past ten

Quarter past two

Quarter past twelve

Quarter to seven

Quarter past four

Quarter to six

Quarter to two

It takes Sandy 15 minutes to walk to school every day. She leaves home at 9 o'clock. What time will she reach her school? Draw the time on the clock and write the answer.

Answer _____

It is 10:30. Lily's friend told her to meet her at the park in 15 minutes. Draw the time on the clock when Lily and her friend meet.

Answer _____

Bill finished his homework at twelve o'clock. It took him 15 minutes to finish his homework. What time did he start his homework?

Answer _____

GIFTED

Counting by 5s

5	10	15	20	25	30	35	40	45	50	55

Write the Missing Numbers

5		15		25		35		45		55

	10		20		30		40		50	

5				25				45		

5			20				40			55

5					30					55

Example

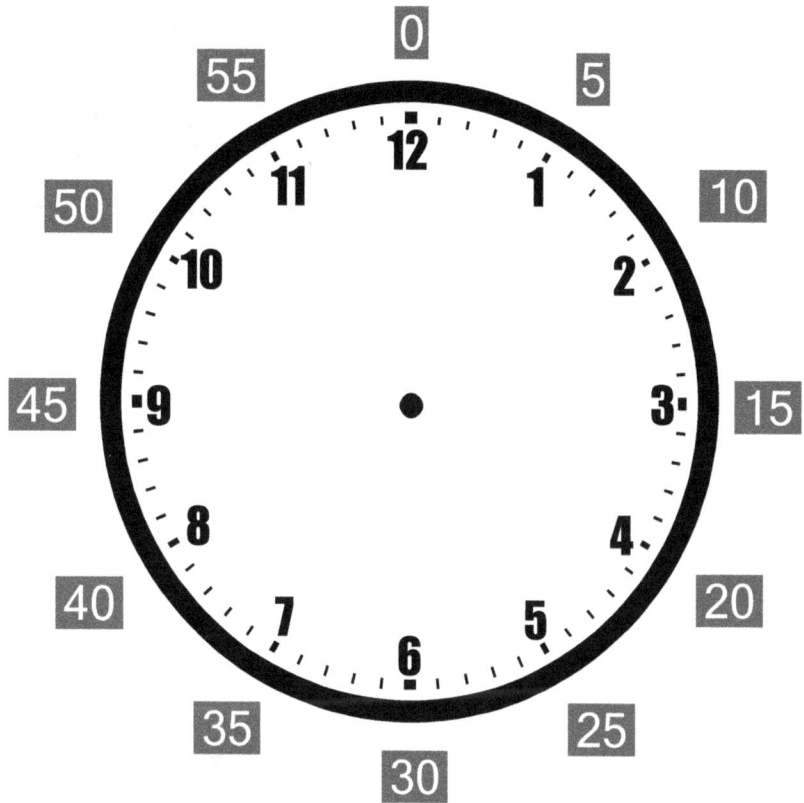

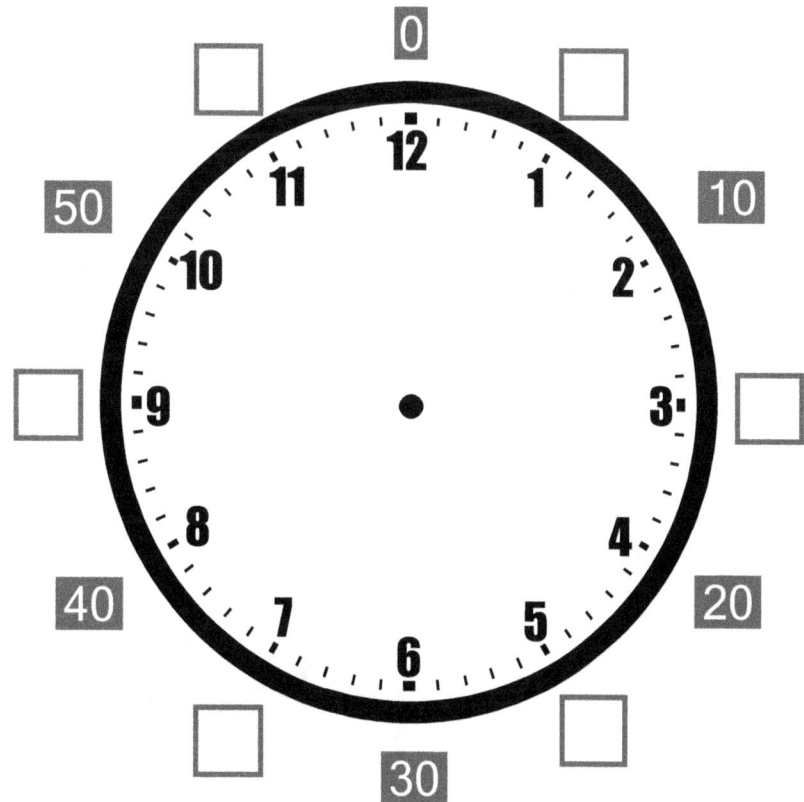

Fill in the boxes with the correct numbers. Count by 5s to find the answer.

Counting by 5s

0

45 **15**

30

55 **5**

40

25

:00

The minute hand is at 12

It is 00 minutes past the hour

The time is 1:00

:05

The minute hand is at 1

It is 5 minutes past the hour

The time is 1:05

:10

The minute hand is at 2

It is 10 minutes past the hour

The time is 1:10

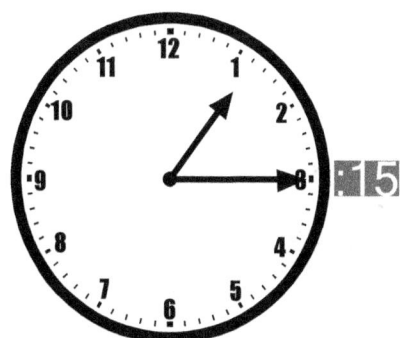

:15

The minute hand is at 3

It is 15 minutes past the hour

The time is 1:15

The minute hand is at 4

It is 20 minutes past the hour

The time is [ ]

The minute hand is at 5

It is 25 minutes past the hour

The time is [ ]

The minute hand is at [ ]

It is 30 minutes past the hour

The time is 1:30

The minute hand is at [ ]

It is 35 minutes past the hour

The time is 1:35

The minute hand is at [ ]

It is 40 minutes past the hour

The time is [ ]

:40

The minute hand is at [ ]

It is 45 minutes past the hour

The time is [ ]

:45

The minute hand is at [ ]

It is 50 minutes past the hour

The time is [ ]

:50

The minute hand is at [ ]

It is 55 minutes past the hour

The time is [ ]

:55

The minute hand is at ☐

It is ☐ minutes past the hour.

The time is ☐

The minute hand is at ☐

It is ☐ minutes past the hour.

The time is ☐

The minute hand is at ☐

It is ☐ minutes past the hour.

The time is ☐

The minute hand is at ☐

It is ☐ minutes past the hour.

The time is ☐

Practice

The minute hand is at [ ]

It is [ ] minutes past the hour.

The time is [ ]

The minute hand is at [ ]

It is [ ] minutes past the hour.

The time is [ ]

The minute hand is at [ ]

It is [ ] minutes past the hour.

The time is [ ]

The minute hand is at [ ]

It is [ ] minutes past the hour.

The time is [ ]

The minute hand is at ☐

It is ☐ minutes past the hour.

The time is ☐

The minute hand is at ☐

It is ☐ minutes past the hour.

The time is ☐

The minute hand is at ☐

It is ☐ minutes past the hour.

The time is ☐

The minute hand is at ☐

It is ☐ minutes past the hour.

The time is ☐

Clock 1
- ☐ 3:05
- ☐ 10:20
- ☐ 8:55
- ☐ 4:45

Clock 2
- ☐ 3:10
- ☐ 7:20
- ☐ 12:05
- ☐ 1:30

Clock 3
- ☐ 8:50
- ☐ 9:25
- ☐ 6:35
- ☐ 4:45

Clock 4
- ☐ 5:20
- ☐ 7:40
- ☐ 12:10
- ☐ 9:10

Clock 5
- ☐ 3:35
- ☐ 7:50
- ☐ 9:50
- ☐ 4:50

Clock 6
- ☐ 7:40
- ☐ 7:55
- ☐ 9:25
- ☐ 1:05

Clock 7
- ☐ 9:05
- ☐ 8:40
- ☐ 5:35
- ☐ 4:35

Clock 8
- ☐ 3:00
- ☐ 7:10
- ☐ 12:30
- ☐ 6:05

Choose the Correct Time

1.
- [ ] 9:05
- [ ] 10:40
- [ ] 1:25
- [ ] 4:10

2.
- [ ] 8:45
- [ ] 5:50
- [ ] 9:30
- [ ] 1:15

3.
- [ ] 4:40
- [ ] 9:15
- [ ] 6:55
- [ ] 4:35

4.
- [ ] 5:25
- [ ] 6:20
- [ ] 2:25
- [ ] 9:40

5.
- [ ] 3:45
- [ ] 3:30
- [ ] 12:25
- [ ] 1:10

6.
- [ ] 4:50
- [ ] 12:05
- [ ] 7:30
- [ ] 1:10

7.
- [ ] 3:15
- [ ] 10:55
- [ ] 5:40
- [ ] 4:35

8.
- [ ] 3:20
- [ ] 7:00
- [ ] 3:20
- [ ] 4:40

Choose the Correct Time

1.
- [ ] 3:05
- [ ] 12:15
- [ ] 8:55
- [ ] 4:45

2.
- [ ] 8:45
- [ ] 5:50
- [ ] 2:15
- [ ] 1:15

3.
- [ ] 8:50
- [ ] 9:25
- [ ] 3:35
- [ ] 4:45

4.
- [ ] 5:30
- [ ] 6:20
- [ ] 2:25
- [ ] 9:40

5.
- [ ] 4:25
- [ ] 7:50
- [ ] 9:50
- [ ] 4:50

6.
- [ ] 4:50
- [ ] 12:05
- [ ] 7:30
- [ ] 1:20

7.
- [ ] 5:15
- [ ] 7:20
- [ ] 11:25
- [ ] 2:05

8.
- [ ] 9:20
- [ ] 7:05
- [ ] 5:40
- [ ] 8:10

Circle the Correct Answer

3:35 | Example

5:35

8:45

9:10

Circle the Correct Answer

12:15

4:25

10:40

1:20

Write the Time Below each Clock

Example

The hour hand is not at 11, but just before 11. The minute hand is at 11, so the time is 10:55

3:

:20

5:

:10

3:

:

:

:

:

:

:

:

Write the Time Below Each Clock

GIFTED

Telling Time for Grade 1
79
JAYCLAD PUBLISHING

Draw the Minute Hand

Example

2:25

The time is 25 minutes past 2. So the minute hand should point to 5

1:10

1:20

2:15

3:20

3:35

4:25

7:20

5:30

4:40

5:35

6:05

6:35

7:40

8:45

8:55

9:50

9:10

12:15

10:40

10:55

12:05

3:55

1:35

2:40

10:05

9:50

5:15

7:25

6:15

4:20

3:10

12:35

Fantastic

1:10

3:20

7:40

3:35

2:25

9:30

12:05

1:20

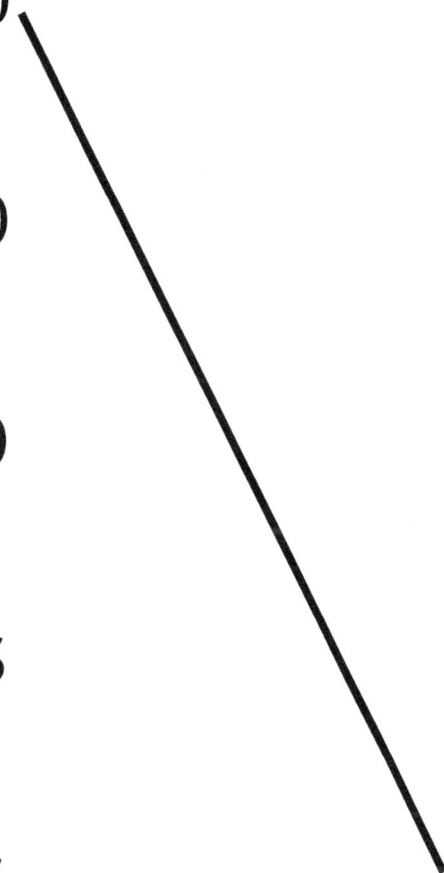

Word Problems

? Andy's piano teacher comes to his house at 5:35 every day for piano lessons. Draw the time on the clock.

? Brian leaves for school at 7:40 every day. Which of the clocks shows the time that he should leave for school?

☐   ☐   ☐

? Christine's favorite TV show starts at 6:35 every night. Draw the time on the clock when the show will start.